Musca Domestica

Musca Domestica

CHRISTINE HUME

INTRODUCTION *by* HEATHER MCHUGH

BARNARD NEW WOMEN POETS SERIES

BEACON PRESS
BOSTON

Beacon Press
25 Beacon Street
Boston, Massachusetts 02108-2892
www.beacon.org

Beacon Press books
are published under the auspices of
the Unitarian Universalist Association of Congregations.

05 04 03 02 01 00   8 7 6 5 4 3 2 1

This book is printed on acid-free paper that meets the uncoated paper
ANSI/NISO specifications for permanence as revised in 1992.

Text design by Preston Thomas
Composition by Wilsted & Taylor Publishing Services

Library of Congress Cataloging-in-Publication Data
Hume, Christine.
    Musca domestica / Christine Hume ; introduction by Heather McHugh.
        p.   cm.—(Barnard new women poets series)
    In English.
    ISBN 0-8070-6859-4 (pbk.)
    I. Title.   II. Series.
PS3558.U438 M87   2000
811'.54—dc21   99-087864

for ERIC ELSHTAIN

They seek no wonder but the human face.

CONTENTS

Introduction by Heather McHugh xi

True and Obscure Definitions of *Fly,* Domestic and Otherwise 3

Helicopter Wrecked on a Hill 7

Highway Address 8

Notes from the House Sitter 9

Map Drawn from Memory by My Brother 11

Lies Concerning Speed 13

Fifty-two Weeks 14

Total Things Known about Motion 15

The Hummed Space between Marooned and Migration 18

Various Readings of an Illegible Postcard 19

Dialogue of Thunder 20

Steps to Entering the Whole Feeling 21

Report 22

Found between Flyleaf and Title Page in Florence Nightingale's
Notes on Nursing, Second Edition 23

[on the other side] 24

Welcome the Desert Bandit 25

A Million Futures of Late 26

Interview 28

A Thin Pissing Sound 30

Mimicry 31

Regard the Horse's Feet from Behind 35

Old Song Keeps Arriving 36

Extracted Gravity 37

Evolving Laws 38

Foghorns 39

Circumference 40

Ladder 43

Sick 47

A Spell in 839 Letters 48

Articulate Initials 49

Idea for an Echo 51

Without Prejudice or Intent: A Survey of Long Distance 52

Aimee under Icicles 54

On Our Way to Meet Your Body Bag 55

Abridging the Correspondence 56

The Mistaken 57

Oak Avenue under the Magnifying Glass 58

Occupied Foundation 60

Miraculous Panoptic Precipitations 61

Echolocation 62

Licked: A Domestic Tale 63

Town Legend: Keeping Well 65

Called Up to Carpenter a New Tradition, We Make Use
of a Standard Round Table 66

i. The Glass Is a Hand 68

ii. A Headlight Is the Gaping 69

iii. Glass and Water Light a Fan 70

Notes: Fly Paper Palimpsest 73

Acknowledgments 75

INTRODUCTION

Christine Hume's opening whirl of *OED* citations is a collage of welcome, an introduction to a theme. "I will fly you a line," she promises—and fly us a line she certainly can. The inventive intelligence at work in this winging shining work ultimately itself becomes the tenor of the ubiquitous fly-figure—like the kind of "voracious winkler" Valéry says vision is. For the theme is no less glinting than are its variations—a dazzling array of guises and disguises, calculated (in canny intermittencies) to give a reader a good buzz.

Consider the remarkable poem "Helicopter Wrecked on a Hill." Its figures are prolix: "a tail chasing / its dog," "the film reel of a plantation / of sophisticated blades," "shades of halos, from your mounted, / swinging factory, cobra-coiling zeros / like a lucky number," "the baton girl . . . twirling her first rib," and so on. Ultimately, however, these turnings aren't just superficial. The poem that begins with "you spin the illusion of rescue" ends with "the good world"—so we know that a participant in at least one reading is the planetary whirler itself. With its lickity-splits of visual analogy, the poem is a festival of spokes. Only in retrospect are the darker implications of the title's "wrecked" remembered, so we wind up sensible of the seriousness of all its gearshifts of scale. It's not just the life of each vehicle that Hume investigates for dazzle: it's the vehicle of each life.

So "Helicopter Wrecked on a Hill" offers us a microcosm of the book itself. Its range is virtuosic—its formal and figural vehicles veer here and there in lively inventiveness, velocity, variety. Seldom has a first book attempted so many stylistic adventures in language. At the heart of the book is a series of poems whose secret charge, like lightning bolts from Mercury or Pegasus, has everything to do with meaning's own metric: a reader on this wild ride must at the very least re-understand the status of a footnote. A poem like "Idea for an Echo" can thus be many things at once: a love poem, a death-study or necromancy, an ironist's reading of the evidences of spirit, and an actual example of intellectual architecture. The form of Hume's intelligence is plastic, periphrastic, Protean. Its virtuosities are exercised with uncommon rhetorical and referential energy. The combination gives off terrific convective force.

In emphasizing how well-minded are these poems, I don't mean to set Hume up as merely a calculating craftsman, a heartless artisan: there are extremely moving love poems among her characteristically kinetic etudes. She's no sucker—no anthropomorphist, either. She pays attention past the first figure, well into the umpteenth: a form of clarity in the face of the human predicament. So the book that began with "They seek no wonder but the human face" ends with the terrifying line "Even flies come to the eyeball for food." It takes a strange delectator to endure that thought, bear that creature-truth, and a goodly power in a seer to see the larger futures through such local features. Christine Hume's dream-reader is invited to share in just so strange and powerful a delectation.

Heather McHugh
Seattle, WA

Musca Domestica

True and Obscure Definitions of Fly, Domestic and Otherwise

Do what we can, summer will have its flies
a paper fly cage dangles from the ceiling
a fly on the coach wheel
sent her away with a fly in her ear
That fly setteth her upon corrupt things
— in the ointment, — in the soup, — on the wall, — off the handle
He grasps the wand that causes sleep to fly
an egg deposited in her flesh
hence to taint secretly
the flye-slow houres
In a pianoforte, in a screw-log
Then flyes in his face all his whoring, swearing, and lying
as if such colors could not fly; a fire—
a bar— and a butter—
something used to cover or connect
with fingers: nimble as knapping a fogle with fingers fly
under that name we comprehend all
muscarius or fly-killers
appeared in the fly-state in —time
and the infinite swarms do shine
a —taker, a —maker as in Every man his own fly-maker
a familiar demon, a flatterer
with wings to be twisted by hand
of a limb: there you see this vain and senseless Flyer
a —breeder, a —duster, a —fancier
of money: to be rapidly spent
as in herds of fly-bitten meat
the steamship flying signals of distress
the pains wander, shoot, and fly about
as Friday flies over my outer wall
the high arc of a ball that has been struck
and suspends a belief in speed
in the time when flies are to be met with
in the time when flies trouble the long tails of giraffes

on the fly; of birds: to issue forth in a body
at the entrance of a tent

Immediately when I hear I will fly you a line

Helicopter Wrecked on a Hill

Proving again that posture is everything,
you spin the illusion of rescue
and departure's threat, throned pilgrim.
You call yourself *turbine* and *windmill*
banking on science and nostalgia alternately
as you whine your way back into scenic routes,
a hollow and heroic riff.
Imagine our need for your remedy:
beginning life anew, a tail chasing
its dog. A push lawn mower turns over
its one fresh-cut gimmick.
Yet you wink like a plate licked clean
as your anchor unravels its line
and takes up the film reel of a plantation
of sophisticated blades. What they could do
to divide our view into slices
while wheeling it all together
with addition and multiplication crosses,
carrying all we believe.
With centrifugal bliss
you unscrew life-or-death promises
and whirl off your many veils,
shades of halos, from your mounted,
swinging factory, cobra-coiling zeros
like a lucky number or a tally
of wasted time and tired intent,
running up the bill while the wind
cannot be counted on to blow.
Still, the baton girl goes on, proud head
of the parade twirling her first rib,
giving and giving her gift to the good world.

Highway Address

And yet we thought our presence changed it: the sod we laid in tiers like bricks and the birds our dogs planted at stick crosses as the passing lights wore holes in our couches and faces. We were something to look at. We watched their cycles shut around us. We named where they were going—fuming as they were to get there—to the great invisible fortresses and life-times of coming to the kingdom, kingdom come. Very well, the distracted mind is a patient animal waiting for dark to jump the fence like the hitch-hiker we would have picked up, but we are a house. He was tinged with the baseness of darkening blue. The sun behind him cranked bolts of an-cient nerve and laughter. Falling rocks are a hitchhiker's hazard, though some say the rock is only happy when hitting home. So it was with us. Lightning yellowed our teeth like the road's wishing line. Speed orga-nized our air, a force on a field that had not forgotten the forest. It had pull with us.

Notes from the House Sitter

Is it usual? The rodents, they left.

At wet windows I linger. And I become quiet,

absorbed and absorbing the unlikely life

of winter breath measuring then stringing off

bedrooms for incidental characters. My foundation poured,

small bones arrange into a new kind of pet.

Fog families begin meeting with steaming fields.

I become quiet, inhabited by white; quiet because

no one speaks out to quiet me; not that I have nothing to say,

for I might have shouted "summer corn grows here."

Antimatter the shape of an ear bone slips away into deaf air

and the grand tour looks like this:

kitchen's view of headlights, ceilings' views of floors,

entry's rough-walled milky way soon to be rubbed smooth

and dirty around light switches. I'm quiet because it's dark,

because the hands over our eyes are my own.

A here-sided sanity scoffs at the sign about trespassing.

But nothing shakes, nothing rustles through me,

no singing erupts: no note light enough

as I want to be, to float out of the very lap of this estate,

to pass over my own housing. The comet of quiet tails me,

heavy as the bricks' will to be wet clay, tired hands.

I lean against a wall not there but wanting to be seen.

Map Drawn from Memory by My Brother

The tiger strikes, what will man not do?
The fly rises: Where will man not fly to?

This is the same archaic vista as the next with the inside and outside of
the city reversed. A draft
on the wall shows houses floating on water: "Water," he says, "makes it
comprehensible to us."

A dog barking separates the home from its lake reflection; a doubling of
unknowns builds a
skyline for the city; the city is a portrait of insistences; its profile is half
urn.

"It's a quotation," he says. See the heat on his name written large? Behind
it is a mirage the size
of a rearview mirror; the shrubs faintly flayed, hemispheres falling.

In a field of gravitational anomalies, a twin dies of a disease from the
Middle Ages. He takes the
legend literally:

To say the crocodiles and crane flies are decoration is to say they attract
mates. To say they are
armor is to hide the compass in the hungry bird's blind spot.

"Head off in any direction," he says. West is marked by a sky dropping
conversations and
footsteps, a music please turned down.

An early hill-sign takes the form of a profile he thinks is his own but it isn't
only: hundreds of
arches carry a marbling, the clouds inside his body rearrange themselves.

What key are we in? The thief of scales was here. An accomplice could
   not remember something
so fast. "Once we get there the relief itself must be reinterpreted," he says.

We are afraid to follow one of its false escapes: nobody could stand
   roadside with six run-over
rabbits in that heat; nobody could hold herself miniature for long.

Have you noticed how everything comes in pairs? Even on the body he
   has, he has a face. Even
the landscape painting gives clues on hiding from the simplest eye.

Lies Concerning Speed

say a lake decayed: say wind makes a lake of eyes: an eyed lake sees her here: at bottom a lair of cars: broken windshields rise in lambent announcement: lashed and crack attract each other: greenish bubbles microphone her voice: lake of lapped and insides: say it's ventriloquism: against a lake's static: a lotic laziness to list after: look how the stars open frogs: catch a sound to give back in her own voice: say lost red rings, foreign coins, and hair bands: the day face down on a sleeve of swallows: the lake looks hard: shrinking the sky like a muscle: lake of remembering dark nipples, net bones: all the mossy boats marooned: say the way the wind wants it: a shallow mouth trying to dig itself out: but she is built into: is become as sounding glass: lake of stealing and hulls: guess how leaves leave the shapes of wings: a stick bends sound in water: shadows skim the skin debris: mumbling her into shape: say her brain needles when she looks into the edge: lake of dumb and numberless sight: the lucid parts only reflect: still saying how to keep herself overheard: *I could show you myself were I near you*

Fifty-two Weeks

She put a new construction on the water:
the jack of spades from a foreign deck
trumps her postcard's lake. She sends
a flash card of analogies.
Siamese truncheons are to her spidery script
as the alien crown is sistered its reflection
and does not witness itself: the obedience of two
at the table, a kitchen saga seen through a keyhole.

She drops the deck in front of me.
I shuffle wild arrangements,
the sound of feet on the stairs.
She cuts. In my hands, firmly,
are two ends of a volley of arguments
and oaths. I shuffle layers of pulp
feathering gossip: *it's old*
and it's old it's new and given it's new.
As if pumping something
about to burst, I shuffle—
the pulse of a hand that waves,
spades open the sky. Our eyes hold
marble air like a monument between us,
her hand moving back smaller
and smaller until the measure
can no longer be governed
or marked or exactly matched.

Total Things Known about Motion

Flowering plants go feral; fish make holes in the water—they are the naive motions. No rain then or any time falling: nothing called movement because there's nothing but strings of music rising, a halo trying to be whole and wild. The world's blurriness forces out everything else, loads our eyesight. Then our ears quicken to meaning and unmeaning sounds. That way we were going higher, staying light. There is a legend told in guidebooks, but our driver told it as he had always heard it from a child:

> Ice stills branchings so that the skaters
> May rewrite them all day.
> At the edge of the pond, she sweeps the village
> All night from her mouth.
> An albino bear from the corners of her eyes.
> To keep quiet, her brother infests a log;
> The woods, breath-threaded.
> Water quick beneath the ice, drawn by a larger body.

Later, two motions, the rotation and the traveling, divide us. To animate a toy is to initiate a world—a rotation. To lie is to initiate a world—a traveling. Wheel, our only and most lovely lie. All right, here are more: *Lum in Lum Lake means standing water and to sail as in Sail Wheel is to circle round.* The circle is regular and quick about it. Wheel is not a whirlpool, but a home-coiling, and not a red electric burner, either. Let's admit we migrate. That the mystery comes with speed. Sometimes a body of water helps. The map is the inside of an animal opened. A red tree in a stained glass window is broken then reassembled by an unseen hand every year. This tempts a map into sight-seeing.

> music is motion heard
> you're getting closer
> the residue of ringing
> your ears' thirst for celerity
> the sky streaking with hairs
> peculiar in their spasm
> galloping through and under pulse

you're getting warmer
as the ground loses definition
booking up headlong
your shadow unleashes a sudden hole
the idea of gravity
stampedes a cliff of loose rock
still warmer
you take up the music's slanting
and strandedness
the little pieces that get there alive
she answered yes without hesitation

We are like a village frozen at the bottom of a lake. Our town is dying and we need another: above us there is a town borne to air too stupid to stop us. We demand it because we are motion sick. Having learned early that *thin ice will bear a skater who moves quickly*, we go full-blown into the knotty above: we ride our little gust of nervousness up.

Motion erases us like that, drags off memory
And swallows the house entire.
Hands are hardest to cure.
Their Ouija-speed jerks around the alphabet
Because all motion is a sign like handwriting
That wants to save us from hover.

He sees the edges of wind in the red shift of dust. He wears fatigues and cannot remember motion. All day he is hiding with rolled rugs and moving boxes. I see him in jutting angles, but can't tell if he's flat or round. He is zeroing where wilderness increases. One time our brother walks backwards all day, and no one else in the house can move. We can't find him to say stop. In the house we will do these things; it's an ability. Right now whoever is speaking calls forward, back, is lost.

you're ancient again, asleep,
erect, and like a curtain,
static hushes through your sway
and catches the swim
of your golden mouths
where long ecstatic guesses
unhinge the hallways

until the speed of night wishes you
past wishing for
good luck is it bad love
to key for the unexpected
sea you don't mind the sea
of grass for taking you:
a want in the eye is to be lied to

Someone goes around town saying *the idea of movement is a material also.* But mostly it's not; movement is an ancestry: sunlight on the laps of distant dresses, catching the flutter of a bird once trapped in this room and ignoring it. The way we see stars quiver is a glimpse at an ancient avalanche, the memory of heads shuddering in anticipation. Someone can go around town saying anything all she likes.

once the car stops
woods keep wheeling through her
lawns barreling on
unreeled frames vying for
her body takes over
over-taken speed, ghost motion
guns through her for days
like the laughter of like-mindedness
on benches they can't see her
laughter
driven to lengths
laughter
quickens under a streetlight
laughing
glints from the stressed spokes

We used to think speed was a heat, an intimacy we couldn't shake, and we clocked ourselves when we ran around the electric fences' freeze. We'd point to the sky with a glassy look, web it with dates. Hand over hand, we'd cut the ruck of horned waves in time. Then we stopped going out at all. Our herringbones accelerated faintly. Our babies were senile. Our flies grew fat and woozy. Birds began trying to rise away from the carrying sounds. We nodded. A prophet wrote "dig here" on the pavement outside a building guarded with lions. What does the lion mean, half his body sunk in the wall, half his body rushing from it?

The Hummed Space between Marooned and Migration

I am climbing into sidewalk-mica charging a bus window.

I am climbing into a bicycle's blur across an ornate door full of names.

I am climbing into the knees of a swinging girl.

A heart is a bird up there I am climbing into.

I am climbing into the coughing, the man handling a dozen roses.

Humming, I am climbing into my own red humming.
The way I keep my organs separate is by singing,
    and I swallow information the way I do not understand.

I am climbing through a transom into a blank melody finger.

I make rooms and years left when he plays piano,
    leaking a counter-coolness through three bullet holes.

Become wet garden paths rushed through the constellated.
I am a blind engine climbing. I am essaying—my aid is error.

Various Readings of an Illegible Postcard

Horny or Harm seems an ordinary home.
Or Having seen the orchard and hives,
I'm satisfied I've picked the dark pocket
pink or satisfied, pickled larks protect the jinx.
You know I'm trouble with Dixie cups, croquet
and wicker or humble with desire for (cough)
the wicked. Ago? A queer little dog grazing
or gazing lives in my room or ivys my nous.
They have a saying here about your duct-taped boots
or They keep savvy bees in case the butcher balks
which is not cool is nautical is nonsensical.
Attention trick eye! A tension trickles
or After swimming we found the housekeeper dead.
I sing or swing, Let's keep her dear!
All day an unmade bed. One day I'll be young or
going as he who homesteads in foreign castles
deserves or whose domain feigns, casts designs
say, like shadows on the outhouse door or
the outskirts humoring me or out-skirting rumors
last as long as keeping honey
or homey or phone me, money?—Yours

Dialogue of Thunder

Dropped off the tip of the tongue
Or the mind's muddy backslide, a place called
Forgot keeps her listening to downflights,
Laundered lightning's tuning-
Fork-hum of parents still at work on her.

Rubber gloves poised for recondite
Ransacks, their yellow, crooked fingers pass,
Counterpass, stunning her nimble senses.
Fat chance of catching their alarm
And high-toned gravy running with the news.

Their leisure is all industry to her.
Humdrum, they flex near her shaken chimney;
God-eaten spaces spring with experience
And know-how, chanting *Likewise-Likewise. Child,
Don't look at us through your dirty bangs.*

What purview she has stutters.
See how confusing her one body is,
See-sawing on the hinge of house and home.

Steps to Entering the Whole Feeling

You are a lover of the centerpiece. You love the trigonometries
Of no focal point: one blasted wood in three arrangements.
Add branches covered in moss. Add the blankness of evening

Because the unadorned always subject the adorned to their proofs.
Were wood birds, this stick would be an American Eagle with eggs.
But what do birds know of invisibility? Add water to suggest chase.

Call up movement by shifting one thing;
All else holds way, wrought with loosestrife and drift:
It's human to look at a nymph figure beyond the frame.

Birds repeat what they know of your three-sidedness.
Add more wind-pitted shells and stones.
Think of a story you've told now, a sound destroying vertigo.

Remember you cannot rest in that room.
Remember how you came late, and the day had already
    become multiplied,
Differentiated, arranged into confusion? (Didn't you see it sky the sum?)

Remember things must have their sad jugs in the dark.
The wood grain might reveal two animals too full of each other,
Or an ornament dangling a twisted glare: once it sees you as face,
    you have come.

Report

They are all giants for their kind, drenched dark green growing on the cords of drift and dead wood. The common people living nearby call them "Fauses in Flessche," and use them as a cure for amnesia. Some say the clergy of the town have bred them on the sly so they may dine on meat during fast—a flesh of fruit born. These are off-shoots you may wish to pursue. Once the fruit is picked and eased open with thumbs, the juice runs wild with the frightened faceful who has no desire, it turns out, to be born to the surface of day.

Ripened, the fruit becomes buoyant and takes on the colors of a fire. These are the pod-bearing plants, mind you; they pick up dirt and trash in the water. They move like phantasmal adjustments of weather. The pit goes to pith then turns to chittering face. Some of the fruit are pitiless. Put your ear to the vine grown bright sometime; you will want to join but you are too big and bodied.

As for eating, the fruit is divine, and the face is said to be sweet if tough; most prefer to mouth the eyes: no stares, no noise. Lately, however, drown fast or fly seems to be their style.

An index of reported face lives:

> *is put to slow death by child*
> *voices regret of newspaper misprints*
> *founds a covenant for their retreat*
> *shows regard for human accounts of miracles wrought by the body*
> *commits suicide by drowning*
> *erects a tribunal for the trial of facelessness*
> *turns into miniature swan, butchers flock; distinction of, into*
> *vulgar and ascetic*
> *pouts and slouches*
> *hums a certain Finnish folk song which attracts swarms of midges*
> *envies the situation of our bridge of boats.*

No one knows the life-span undisturbed on the tangling vine. The driftwood is often broken up for kindling in the town where how many I can't tell you have seen gloriously tiny faces wheezing in their hearths.

Found between Flyleaf and Title Page in Florence Nightingale's Notes on Nursing, *Second Edition*

—it loves to multiply in small places, in trays of light coming under steps of the staircase. Once we got rid of our hospital's corners, I kept running into your numerical air in fantails and fernings. It nearly plots itself before my eyes, I've only to climb the Crimean curve of wind again or those Indian statistics to get that swell. The great bat's wing of army graves shadows my rounds, but this is uncharted air. And then—sun eating at the window, the sky drifts like a lazy eye. When I walk out, my whites turn: there must be a structural need to become unaccountable, disorganized as disease. You have doubtless heard of such a thing. On your youngest's skin you've seen a fire blown from night air; you said she falls to her knees at every frond in the gravel, but adores more the red numbness of her gravel-pitted knees. Make it into diagram K with tiny figures that she may carry on her breath. Where does all the mouth's moisture go? These beds are swamps, and swamps are likely to go on expressing— a febrile and bloated emotional life hangs over these men, yet they won't know it, the way no one notices a gray pigeon on a stone ledge until, in flight's sixteenth memory, it becomes Nike. Victory there. Victory that. You might have guessed—gangrene is our sudden sickness: like begetting like; the offspring of unclean that sullies blood good, the bullet and buck that ride about in a beautiful place. At night, the ward is quiet with the ocean of wet-breathing, and I listen to see each syllable rise as a man talks nonsense in his sleep. Or recites Persian poetry. Or prays for a brass bird with red glass eyes. Wind animates three ruined aviaries outside his window—he can see the work fever will do on him. A woman leaning over his bed is the only apology.

[on the other side]

This delirium, designed glass-hard yet intimate—the toy prizes inside sheer molecules that cannot animate themselves; one hundred women's worsted work that cannot learn or bloom. Proof: If 109 stray cats trickled through the ward, they could not be dogs on their way out into the moon hue. Do books run the risk of changing into the books they are shelved beside? The nomenclature of atmosphere casts no plastic punch—a fleet fluenza. Heat is a soldier's uniform here, it burns away like cotton. Have you seen a soldier exhaust himself into a radiant cloud? A bogey burnt out of excess. Descriptions of air are not enough. Air is water, air is ice that needs the desert sun of William counting.

Welcome the Desert Bandit

Four calendars but no clock
except my own plans for robbing this place,
more baroque by the hour—Where
would I run?—when you stumble in
with heat coming off you like awkward water.
I call you Fatigue and you're delirious;
even the ants look long-legged
in this air, clear and bright as onions.
Just try and see through it. From the tower
I show you the mirages we hunt,
their fatty humps are an afternoon
of hallelujahs shading the romance
against whatever's picked clean.
To stand beside them is to gain a grammar—
but nothing like when the helicopter lowers
our annual ten-foot floe
and we drum piano tunes for the sun—
forgive us—and the old feel free to spit.
My brothers, sisters and I
lie under its glassy pool
sinking; the first drop
unlocks our sun-bitter faces.
We soak ourselves with happy, wet cussing,
wait to be the last lucky one
to roll up from under it, seaming the sand
that tolerates us evenly.

A Million Futures of Late

There'll be no town-going today;
I'll be wind-rattled and listen
to the window's answering racket.
I'll watch flies manifest from glass
rub the runt and ruthlessness off.
I'll have my lapses into slapsticks
of accent and stutter, girl and mother.
Today flies will spin crowns of woozy cartoon stars for me.
I'll roll my eyes back thinking;
I'll be the picture of flightiness today.
Assumptions will spill from my ears—
a brain storming out in furious herds;
all summer my brain will be a pasture
of tall, hissing grass, a sibilance intent on rising to character air.

Fly forgeries of *z* wallpaper my room: chain saws, prop planes, wind forcing itself through. It's a fact that the skull makes room for the brain by talking; the brain shakes from a curse in the cranium as something dark crawls out of my mouth. The radio is pouring weather I must knit into a shawl. Evenings require a shawl and the wrong love, the wrong noise of one's wrong thinking. Flies come to brain every last inkling into swarm, into arias of amnesia and treble thoughts. No one can shoot something that small.

I'll just shoot off today; I will
blurt out argot in the rawest haze.
I'll be snoring at the kitchen table
while the radio slips into passing traffic.
I will be sworn by. I'll be clairvoyant
by keeping half in the dark. I'll fathom
apropos out-posts by staying home today,
by haunting my own enlarged attic
under worried clocks drum-humming
me down to make me one of their vernaculars—believe me,

black hole, you bright microscopia,
you know best how long I'll stand
stitching up grass-stained synapses
in devotion to inner commands, whatever the invisibles demand.

Interview

This is a beautiful world, it means what I say.

Were you a child?

I am the same all over. My head, a dark spot, in front of a lamp's glow is an areola and a marrow—itself, a map of the universe.

What do you make of gardens?

Ventriloquism: *you beasts hissing over the face of this dead woman.* Countless tiny blue bees kept in my right arm: The lightness of their stinging, the weight of their frenzy. Their humidity made my hair curl; I had the arm hair of an old man. Their softness whispered me to sleep. In those days I had sleep. Now the scalp blusters and I must tell these ecstasies to the knee. The knee gurgles: write it down; tell it to the eyehole, to the under-tongue's pig-tailed pattern.

What do you do for sleep?

All night I pretend I am leaving the pains, walking away from their house, whistling while I gladly go, until they are a faint dazzle of salt. One might lose me, hiding in some smoky heap, dressed up as an arrow, assuming the vein of tingle. The mite-shaped ache comes to the surface. My tongue pokes the sore gap to stoke fire's high-pitching. There is scarcely any room for more; in every telephone there are ten million tones.

What does your voice sound like?

Crawlers, darters, and clingers; poor, bare forked animals and desquamation tribes. In the photograph of tooth life, you may think you see square lawns, pastel houses from the air. A boiling mouth means cultivated feet, as they say. The same baritone pain of the jiggers or chiggers in my foot seem a hairy caviar, amber blisters. Red puckered *O*s are lipstick prints all over my foot; their one joke is a kissing noise on the floor when I walk.

Where is the story coming from? Is it yours to say?

If today my strands drift on confused fluids, they become fish; if on land, alighted wasps. Their voices hang from my body for seconds before I can't remember them.

Will there be a gift for you at the end of the day?

Nymphs of a tongue worm I traveled to Sudan to gather. To this day the marrara eggs find light in my nasal drippings: radiant. In Thailand, three small metallic moths perched on the perimeter of my eye to nurse tears. What did I want with tears? Little sneezes in my ears, the premonition of fecundities. It's not a sensation I could carry.

Will the landscape grow older with you?

My pet is the phantom breast, as it grows and gives back an echo tuned and turned to its origin. A fist-tight weight, a rock shimmering with its own fluted flows. And over a chevron scar, the phantom breast is often reached for, holding the sheet parallel. So as I sleep, it becomes a bird. A bird throwing itself at human faces.

What do you remember for?

Now the stone-cutters chime in, the bell-tollers. Cicadas pick the cotton out of my ears, and the twines of going-green enwraps my fingers. I will amuse myself with their clamor and heat (I will take no volunteers, no cheerful understanders). When the mind's able to melt the ice of body, this last subterfuge will be a child's jar of simple round worms. An eye worthy of the wandering nematode, Loa Loa. Don't I have the biggest cornea you've ever seen? A retina talented enough to refract infection.

A Thin Pissing Sound

settles on her
scribbles itself   her face against wet dense glass
crying is bad for your face
his keys   on a sleeve
swept—at her
alights on his   (this-this-this)
soundparallel   surfaces   the dresser
crying   for   your face
invents places inside her ear

shipshaping
static zag and stem
the steady   web outreaching
cures presence
hectic lines flirt   unfixed

to place / snags corners
would it say   collision inspires
collusion

crying is bad   your face
in the fold   sidereally   shifting
she can't stop or shock   swivel and shed
roll of every dust   at window's interstice
any thought spares her
xed upon dark increase
suddenspell
forget the mirrored doors

interpreting air is bad for
crying   unravels   unto
shutupshutupshut up shut up

space displays
holds her   indecipherable
sleep   is not hers
crying is thy   naked
zeroing head   of heaven
never seen
brushed away

Mimicry

My fly fretted like a secret
My fly was made flamboyant and right
My fly furnished an alibi
After many pleasing relations, my heckler bride
My fly towards lip gloss and shoddy dim rooms
My fly paid attention, soaked in your Westerns
    and many-minded museums
My fly looked from the original eye
My fly was no action painter, no dandy photographer
    sighing over his sorriest of matters
My fly wanted to be you or to mock you
My fly recorded laughter and told the office I was dying
My fly understood about zeal,
    what a suitcase on the bed meant
My fly burrowed in your hair as if it were trying to love you
For five thousand seconds, my fly begged you to cut it out
My fly was not by heart
My fly back-tracked the puzzling narrations
My fly had been misled
My shrunken raven, my imperfect bee
My fly didn't know what it was until it purred sharply in the dark,
    lighting up the room, until it made the room shake
My fly stayed on the wall and vomited
My fly asked you the way out once,
    Do you remember what you said?
My fly never again complained that a window was too close to see
My fly fell faster
When you looked, my fly hurried to disappear
    into everything sideways grown
My fly was the omniscience of an insanely happy town
My fly traded what can't be ahead
    for what can't go on unrecognized

Regard the Horse's Feet from Behind

the animal itself
       is a broker of breaking into
              the track of a girl's trance

over muscular drums
       that drive blood to fruit
              full of seasons of hover

and come together and
       multiply her if you want
              twice as many things

to understand: go away
       such headedness gets lost
              attends an attention

which lasts as long as
       birds rifling trees
              the impulse of pulse-still

fastens her to sky
       that's rowing as if
              everyone always dies at sea

3.] a hive on fire]open fire
4.] at a horse's head chirring honeys
6. hover]stutter]sugar
7. and]to
8.] no one could see the beach from here
11. headedness]headiness]bullying
15.] filled with *bees of the invisible*
16. fastens]absenting

Old Song Keeps Arriving

from a rock jetty
      five monks ease their hems
           into the river the same
man by the same local bridge
      in German birds are vulgar
           someone says four views
from the tree are all
      we need here remembering
           a beach would be distant
as eyes filling up for the winter
      which freezes our hair with clumps
           of leaves clanking against ice oaks
the whole way home a tern
      passes through watching scores
           its eye descants—the listening
aspect of the bird reveals this
      we ask it for another instead
           and finger its trembling (we ask it)

1 . a rock jetty]broken canoes
2 . ease]erase
5 .] where birds migrate in constellations
9 . a beach would be]the wager as
11 . freezes]promises
13 . home]snow-blind
14 . scores]recalls
15 . listening]guileful
18 .] the leaves storm

Extracted Gravity

Its law lights up a small, shaky globe
      that had been waiting to be pitch
            and all things fall opposite the flash

Several rains at once corrupt us
      moths and rust affront us; one of us leaves
            thunderstruck as the historian clutches her curious heart

A tear too—intellectual thing,
      terrible seed—charges its surplus upward
            triumphing the quick over the good

Tall men stand by trying to help
      one calls down a shabby green light
            yea, he is my lover in the nineteenth remove

And a lover is always staying through
      a storm, until its scroll rolls back
            when I have finally fallen asleep

Until I tell you how the sun rose
      how before that how long held
            round my opening mouth will be

---

1 . a small, shaky globe]my hand
4 . at once], glass-baffled,
5 . leaves]fakes
8 . terrible seed]terrible stone on my tongue—
9 .] *the small raine downe can raine*
14 . rolls back]whispers me my disaster
18 .] low how cold how awful you will be

Evolving Laws

Each lift convinces the centiplume
    to swallow what keeps being sad
        when she became a body

I had to see her
    circulation, I had to see it
        as a mirror, inside its wild

The proof makes another flight
    her moth-talk holds the signature of
        —gray wings in her throat

Revolving as if the key
    to propulsion were a belief
        in vanishing helixed to the brain

Glass jars shake in the dark;
    we eat sugar from spilling handfuls
        because starving requires

Her head stolen, her arm still curved
    against her husband's back
        and quotation marks emptied

Of hand forget to take—
    drafty as singularities, fast
        for her lungs; even then

    2 . to swallow]nothing. That's still
    5 . circulation]plagiarism
    7 . makes]asks
  9–10 . throat/Revolving]voice/Never did alight
    13 .] Blindness in her draft
    19 . take]shape
    20 . drafty]bodiless]elsewhere]alluring
    21 .] verge of her druthers

Foghorns

after Arthur Dove

A gunshot organs the fog, then three blinks
    subtract each other—the (once) red sky behind him arranged.
        He must have been unraveling a cold city's lights.

The only fixed point inside blackens
    like a mouth; the lapping (water) is an accident of muscle
        so that he bends his knees while walking on the world.

Casting for spells and caveats from the yawl,
    his fluent eye holds (something of) a hard wine chant.
        Though his mouth is what he feared:

The heavy axis of that which must give up
    what it makes *real in itself.* The (dumb) glare burns down
        to nothing but aureole handwritten as beehives.

He watches the trance haunting our 291 smoke curls
    and lees in glasses. This is (why) his memory of a meteor
        over an ocean ago in Halesite rings accurately white.

We call into his *gong-tormented* folds;
    a seeing syllable turns (belly) up in his hindbrain.
        The sound assumes we live its ruddy concentricity:

If his grip begins to shake (as he offers). . . .
        If it's beautiful it will poison you.

1 . organs]mirrors
8 . hard wine]burning]red bells
9 .] The mask of moaning a mouth:
11 . glare]buckeye painted on a bowl
15 . an ocean]his cobbled monocle
17 . syllable]favorite cymbal]apple
18 . live]wade out in
19 .] He remembers how fast the sea wills you.
20 . poison you.]be *gift* in German.

Circumference

Degrees must repeat themselves
      for anyone to believe
            bloated ornaments of bees
suspended outside us, whistling
      botches on Bergen Street,
            whole listings of bickers
that skirt the dead thing
      for empties among the rocks—
            vagrancies of one thought
become frenzy, come to
      a closing down, woken in sun
            to show them we have nothing
in our sky but your radii
      bannering exhaust; wrong
            is the flat place we're all
for, we grow larger: you stand
      on a double bridge drunk deep
            in the boneless of periplus once

1 . repeat]disclose
4 . outside]tending
6 . bickers]misheard things
7 . skirt the dead thing]hang dead
10 . frenzy]for good]good for/closing down
11 . in]to
13 . our sky]those laddering filaments
18 . boneless]wild parrots

Ladder

You walk among rocks in the dark;
the phosphorus vaccine is the spot you look for.

You see bright metal in the sky ahead,
windows full of the backs of heads you think into faces,
think when you find phosphorus
you will see the glass startle with eyes.

At night the names of things stick to you—
wet leaves on windows or you dream of a cliff on water
mossed with the vaccine, and the cliff does not sink
when your body tries the water.

Fish, birds, and insects mark place by their motion.
It means the water reflects enough to drink.

There is a picture which shows it: a baby feeds
on a lit breast in the background.

Here is a picture which shows it working: a child undoes
knots in his mother's bleary necklace, strands of silver
on the hard floor.

Virus is a string in a plant.
We get in the way and fall sick.

You did not say the burning thought aloud
or describe the feral place's sudden green—burn it—
to yourself. You did not say white or red but burn it.
You say it whistling along coloring as you burn.

What could be done with enough grant money:
       a. The flesh of victims buried in Siberian permafrost
          could be tested for viral life.

b. Dues to wonderment shooed.
c. A painter paints your sketch of DNA
with phosphorus.
d. All the things would become people.

The cold caught is the story of space asweep,
rocks and tall grasses absorbing your words one by one.

All the same you bring a magnifying glass.

You hear cries of people on a roller coaster falling.
The cries have no sound but are balancing all sound
so that you may walk across the bridge.

Entering the water, you see yourself in the sky.

The city, though it is dying.

If everything here is twinned underground, if the city in fact mirrors
the sky, why don't you look there?

Take cases in the order they came: Rameses V, Pocahontas,
Emperor Gokwomyo, one third of Iceland in 1707.

You remember an old story about being lost:
the self-replicating wood turns you
against your own memory,
rain on the sea becomes sea.

On the volcano, virus is the word for springtime.

You imagine what a letter from the city might sound like as you sift
through the pipes and bricks, and feel the square of red carpet a
tree's bark has grown around.

You are playing a joke on the forest with your quietness.

You will not open your eyes. Your hands will tell you.
You see the vaccine as light on your lids.
Your hands will show it to you.

The city swarms with steps on the point of finding their own tracks.

The world is a staircase just now; you can say things about it that way.

The milkmaid's roughshod hand,
the Broad Street water pump handle
pass through you nightly.
Passaging the virus is an idea instantly
forgotten by one and remembered by another.

But you have never spent time on a farm.

Thinking like that inside a rotten tree trunk.
A germ creates or destroys.

More animal-clues: skeletons in a cave carved out
by elephants looking for salt.

The picture stands for the lit and unlit insects
high-pitched and unfocused in the rock's crevice.

Of the 64 cellular hexagrams, 8 remain unchanged when inverted.
    Beware of insect bites, infected breath, and bad meat.

Even if a woman stares at her girl through the window, she
cannot become the girl. She becomes against the girl.

A child piles glow worms in the shape of the inside of a mouth.
    They steam in rain.

A doll half-sunk in the mud. A porcelain arm lit up like phosphorus.

You begin a concordance for the prehensile hand.
You invent an apprentice to help with your tic and flinch.

At night you talk to the fire, sound inside sound,
and to the water when you finally hear it: sight opening sight.

Will small self-violences inoculate against
the clenched-fist injuries?

The city you walk toward is your own because you have already
reached the sea and turned back.
Glare soaks you; neon splashes words against you.
Turn your attention to stone.

How small is the vitreous vaccine—smaller than a period?

Infection needs a landscape of infection.
It invents its own scale,
too bright to be seen with the human eye.

Under branches you imagine viral tricks:
caterpillar-shape link fetal-shape link bullet-shape link question mark.

The house remembering itself. The body remembering itself as part
    of a house.

The furniture has been rearranged. The original furniture has been
    replaced with near-exact replicas.

You forge a road to the house in your eyes. That is, you try
to remember what became you.

Sick

Sleek-shouldered and clumsy,
your body is painted on a taped bottle,
a network of crafted crack and knot
and torn flags of drying tissue
that baffle the eye. You invent
the medicine of fresh pursuit;
the what's-hiding-in-the-bottle
slinks after you: souvenir, embryo
or precious breath blown into your whistling sleep.
Whistles keep children and drunkards away
from the blood that gorges your sex
and stays all over your face.
And who drew the penis?
Will it never grow dim?—in black marker
on your thigh bent like a strong arm.
Ghosts don't have legs like these
ton of bricks shuttling down,
sluggish and dark as planets.
That's self-cruelty's little talent:
your comfort is kicking the ball hard
and touching yourself afterward.
Don't pick painted and polished tape;
don't look under the shakes deep
drowning in your belly's mean perimeter.
You see outlines and shadows and come up with,
"This is a baby bottle; a punching bag
baiting the Mrs. with its shape." Upright
you dumbly wait for dawn's sugary rim.
Pull away from your slender prison;
coax up your water; pour your
one-way of fierce pleasure,
if for nothing but bone.

A Spell in 839 Letters

Once you had the eyepower to silence backyard animals,
to unbristle them with your homespun beams of salty empathy.
But gravity is peeling down the neighborhood,
so that we soon will be middle-huddled
around a fire and a lake with no dogs. Everywhere
the camouflage of coupling and fresh hybrids crying havoc:
the future in forestlessness is in formation. They burn
kingdom corners and move on, adopting the next vowels
and another feckless attempt at family.
They have their dirty little thirsts, lamps under the lake
opening lidless like mouths. They're beside themselves
as they prepare the peace of human faces in reflections.
Their nostalgia for having once been viruses turns them weird.
As they turn on you—you have dreamt of it for eons, you
in your trance trained on staring them down—
they look at the incoherent above, where you cleave
to wind, to the reds in sky desperate to prove yourself many selves
to chalk up among your geniuses, your greatest lusts,
your everyday ideas of an infinite country.

Articulate Initials

Love, C—he slopes the letter like half of his hip caught in Pompeii;
his fist locked in his pocket or held floating
over the page the way a singer holds a high C, her last note
which aims to be an arrow through the pulse of a heart, a heart with a tail
and sharpened eye, a *pupil* label sticking needle-like
out of the eye, a sun spot, sun breaking through
the tree—lit up
in the brain bearing fruit, a tree
burning to fall as a hole falls
from the sun marking the middle of a sentence,
a comma's little hook flipped
dragging you to the front, fresh from the initial mistake.

The earliest books illuminated initials
by which we could understand the story:
from the start the garden grows like mad;
poisons give off degrees of sweetness;
a *C* fattens into a plumed animal, an *H* writhes
with lizard-dogs on the bark lovers write their initials into,
but our letters would not
separate into distinct daughter cells—
ten scratches which must be little but belong.
We lost the periods fearing each other.
They were the tripping stones, stumps on the garden path,
kick stands to say the letter stands for
standing, for basketing the excess behind, and inside,
door stoppers prop the bedroom ajar.

I am hiding with him there
in his initials; two of us painted on a narrow bed,
but the body won't reduce the way a name will.
I help him make the *H:* stretched out facing him on the bed
even stretch marks, even hairs follow the downward stroke;
an extra arm or leg hung over me as I sleep—
the Hercules constellation, our thickly bordered country,

fat as cartoon lungs crawling with ballpoint flora.
This jointed seeing is not uncommon after sex.
A letter's joint can be a gesture or a flourish
I am articulating as I lie on the bed;
He is separating and converging as he lies.
To articulate is to joint; to joint is to separate, to converge.

His voice moves too as it tries
to hold my whole name in his mouth.

Because I know his name well enough to forget it.
Because he will author the action.
Because he has something of the wink and flirt in him.
Because he is pretending to be reduced or rushed.
He signs the letter *CH* as in chew, as in chant, champ, chump—
the sound of a train's effortful start or a lisping child's request for silence
in the house of firsts, the house he searches with both hands
for bourbon and candy, the house that accelerates the past
the rest of his name runs from, withdraws.

Idea for an Echo

trash blown against	the chain-link fence
reverses the lines	of parasites in a deer's spine
laughter received	into your head
camouflages thin air	the mountain lichenized
a bird's scat into	half fish half house half running
child on a cliff spreads	from a shallow holdfast
the faithless shrub	takes up the map of flowing
and a love of difficulty	grows as deep
as the height of a cliff	which depends on the bird who lives there
What does laughter	*look like when it's entered your body?*
you thought water	curling under ice would be safe
the wet sleeping	between your legs like a hand
Where will you hide	*his voice?*
When does he	*light your ear?*
breath pushes the face	before you into two and you think
one of them	one of them

Without Prejudice or Intent: A Survey of Long Distance

I. SOUNDING OUT

You wanted a voice
from my mouth you wanted
it right; a voice is written,
exciting itself in the dark.
The horizon lowers to let in
more sky, more listening room.

I want to get to the blown glass of early cloud chambers
Put your finger here: Accident inventing us inside

You said you made a sky
that could be read as a face.
You make the night sound
for me. Only your hands
were the names of boats. Listen
to the background repeating itself.

I was trying to learn the language of languishing
Put your ear to it: You believe in everything blown up

Make the sound inside
my mouth imperfect you said
and could only guess why my voice
was spilling sea over your hands.
You couldn't see it that way;
you said that still isn't right.

It used to be that all water was written in red
Look: How the lies become visible to you

The letter comes back a rounded scene

Hold the calligraphy's pitch to your wind-swept face

Its thinking is a hundred flies turning the sky open

Then fallen to your bed sheet

      did he feel for softness in the ribbed and lamped italics
      did he watch the vowels go round in order to see faces
         in them, the rolling of tired type
      so late, did he trace a wingspan thinking a thing or two
         about despair
      did he copy comics just to contain the world in a wall

You follow the sky's lines in your hand

Paper draws the water out of your skin as you scrawl

Heart held in the fifth movement of leap and banking

You cannot believe anything in his horizons

      did he press down hard, did his ink branch out and come to this
      did his voice distort the tracings, did he hear himself
         crumble up *the world is in despair and I alone am happy*
      did his marks make the swallows go blank over water
      did he mispronounce the whole-arm method

What can come from curve is a line to follow

Is a broken seasickness that's come through even frozen ink

A body seeing through then caught inside a light or between

Hold the thinking to you, close your hand around

Aimee under Icicles

Why keep on about the cold? That baldness follows?
                    Maybe this is reassurance: two-bit flags
At the portal, Severeville's frozen petting zoo.
          She takes the haughty halo,
                              Stands for its bright lip.
                              Each drop cops her.
Every hesitation is dealt cold water.
          Cold, she feigns caryatid,
                    Never wedding gesture to an avarice bone.
          Water hesitates on the round
                                        then spits down—
She packs her head high with second-hand ice.
                    A stranger sculpts a beehive there;
                    Children take chips home to their parents.
Look here, she sees clean through all this great glassiness;
          And with giant steps,
                    I hear horses, flames, sugar.
She names men on her fingers and tries to admire her hands.
          Hers is the posture vertigo takes.
Under icicles,
                    skies and seas hold daggers.
Freeze is part of the dark her hand goes to.
          Are you open to it? Are your wide watches empty?

On Our Way to Meet Your Body Bag

We used to listen
for your approach while a mile away
you defaced pennies on the rails.

Your collection was dedicated to the joy
of leveling detail into simple shape and shine,
an edge sharp enough to use.

We could have killed the fly trapped
in our house. The windows open for nothing
but fizz and wave, the night trains' pale parachutes.

We've faced the sky this way before,
on our backs, our bodies not light enough to save
any blade's posture beneath us, not heavy enough to sink.

Now you're in a blue known
to vanish into a starched uniform of iron good will,
lifting its hat, *My car is full, thank you,*

Or *Good game, good game.*
They must be from some new planet, speaking
in exhaust systems while deader flies are dialogued around us.

Abridging the Correspondence

Telling the particles of the clouds, the leaves, the water
What immortality is. That it is immortal.

Your crystalline sentences crack up, loosening their crackle. They ignite
from verbs at their ends and a kind word or two for kindling. For what's
crossed out. Ashy demands cough up their containment—scatter by draft
where a dense, broken script chokes the corners. You've enclosed a pic-
ture of yourself in a new state; you've sent an artful but martial postcard.
Your humor's beyond me. Your run-on veins of nerve exchange easily for
floating fog rings. Your phrases, puffed and opaque, dye my breath. Dear,
I know zero of a smokeless love. And these are the effects that bring down
your address. Earth didn't make this carbon mess—your arabesque ca-
denza. Let it gray armpits and stick to eyelashes, the rest swarms unruly
as lace. I know its strength, a fine resilience, a resolution to cash in a bad
thing. This is how I talk myself out of giving in: "It *is* dead. Like a dead
thing's foaming mouth that won't stop foaming, dead or not." The mean-
est of ashes glows and shakes in the city of lava. That one's my nickname
and postmark in the city of precious little left. I'm emptying out your out-
paced scribble into a corresponding cold. I'm consistent; I do not dis-
solve in water. The surface leaves, turns blue. A bluish exhaust burns in
the blue high of noon: your blank signature, your faintest salutation. I
only mean that you've launched blackbirds straight from your fugitive
gut, and they've flown into fire. The dust of them is enterprising, all rest-
lessness and resentment. This is how you erase the interior: send it up in
a seedy laugh that adumbrates a dumb nothing, a dumb anything ready to
be born.

The Mistaken

Dear Folks, I've gone away for good.
Every gorilla and acrobat here
takes risk for acts of privacy
and too bad if their landings

interrupt a fine growing season
or converting hour
when all the Latin names come to them,
when they blame the standing animals
and secure them to rocks.

No, this isn't a mistake;
you've come and you'll stay.

Stay just off the deck of a dingy stream
where foliage parades its fat lizards
and spring trees are painted on the dark
dry wrinkles of elephants—

Dear Folks, Don't worry
I believe exactly half of everything:
that fatigue is just the kind of clarity
to save this squat acre;
that indifference can be modeled
on their whirl and tumble fervor,

their soaring-drunk songs
in the never-ending rivalry to be on time
to tell children—sleep,
dream up your steady river, your idea
of only two kinds of people, really.

Either way I won't be left.

Oak Avenue under the Magnifying Glass

On fire, the trees do not untangle.
Not one claims itself
in the red-yellow fade and laud.
"Are we the only survivors?" he asks.
Wind blows the fire further. The lovers rehearse,
roll and pat, douse with baking soda,
stay low. Her tired hands
are collar-plattering his head
above the flames; a gem of ice
she tries to find a cool spot for.
Flip the pillow. Open a window.
His beard, his woolly chandelier,
holds a gallon of smoke-heavy water;
a burden she likes. They plan a new table,
an extra chair while they lean
on a ration of phrases. The trail fragment
forces them up a hill. Sap trees
bark at them and offer up a rusty plenty.
Squirrels drop. Pine needles are elastic to their feet
and leave no tracks. "How old are we?" she asks.
They have forgotten the method
of distinguishing each other.
When the heat calls for sweat,
they press together like eyelids.
The air's not thinning.
That smoke is acorns cooking.
What crackles is rain.

There they rest in a round of choices
and don't remember the fire. If the image is blurry,
they stop pitching pennies.

There, doubt is handwritten in lemon juice
over a bypass, under their breath.

They hold up a collapsed bridge:
thousands of minute
bodies flash and drive there and back.

Let's call them brave; tell them
"Just around this corner. . . ."
And when the water is drawn flat, let's build a statue
where they go.

There, they resemble the novel family
and scout among weeds.

There, thunder lights up a hiding place
where they would calculate if not for the smell.

Occupied Foundation

L'Appartamento Dei Nani Mantora,
Mantua, Italy

below hanging floors, the noise of a shadow
swinging as if it were attached, as if birds
know only blue and white paint

the dwarves hear a music of knees on hollow stairs:
that song goes, *the place to see and the place*
to touch are joined by a seam

but the spring vault slips center and both exits dress as dead ends
so the mind invents pleasures, doesn't it,
just to believe in them

they look up between planks and knots at chambers left
for unexpected hours; to touch the ceiling stops
the slide of spied through

every window from one window against which a jester
throws pleated hand plays that no one can
imagine or be amused by

this too is a lit detour: the dwarves wake believing
themselves on a boat to the world; No, one says
it is only singing and be lost

Miraculous Panoptic Precipitations

Rained milk and blood during the courtship
Rained fish and no flesh
Left unplundered by birds went bad
Rained tiny biting mouths
High on the hill rained feedback let it
Rained a stone from the sun which is itself
Stone lording noon
Over us rained clearest at the tail of sleep
Into a gaudy birdbath rained
Sea if sea were up there
You'd tilt your eyes at it and hiss
Counter-drag downing you
Rained Iowa in India
Changed the course of rivers
Arrows rained on bears
One person struck forgot how to read
Rained spelt round the stronghold
And mold upon the skein
Panspermia in your baffled ear once spilled
Sirens splitting night in two
Rained that you had to take bladders out of yourself
Plans for a little canoe
Spilled saliva in a goodly spot
Rained cirrus set on fire rained evaporated vaccines
Sixty god-stiff things bloated the land
What it forgot rained
Chloroform near engorged waters which made a century
Unmade raining so as not to retain
Rained to keep the told not telling
To keep pointing upward pointing
Hand come down
You're chosen to rain now rain

Echolocation

They are giant birds he said ancient moth-eating birds
    face is a theory
After he wire-hung antelope heads in his oak
    words don't give us faces
She draws a speculation of ruminant musculature
    show me the face of here
Upstairs her brother practices violin
    a face unresponsive isn't a face
The soundings in delay stray and circle
    anything that frightens is a face
Ice-smitten, skin-suspicious, horn-sobered
    is a face a lip an eyebrow
Antelope heads rack and fray her winded sight
    movement is the origin of face
This time her brother makes it through to the part he must pluck
    touch or writing completes a face
She could track her way back by snow fences, telephone poles
    faces need to be used because they're unfinished
Her mind takes the shape of three ornaments turning on a tree
    all faces are blind and will-less
Where her face is docent to cages of bent spotlights
    can a face say without a mind
Then the strings run again from the top
    burn dissolves a fixed face
The tree is not a mistake is wingfuls of false eyes

Licked: A Domestic Tale

Prophets never enjoy a Darwinian edge.

Tongue is the cause of my being here. . . . Tongue brought us here and tongue brought you here.

Tiny careers of mushrooms
explode after the flood. Our valley's
happy fecundity doubles half-lives,
yet our hearth will hardly stay lit.
Damp, the musty wares wear on.
And my tongue outgrows me.
While family learns my expressive turns
of the wet cluck and blotting babble,
my brother calls in the town;
he loudly cries in crowds around me:

"In the ditch of her jaw, fungi fathered
a galvanic growth. No clamp or suture
could stop her burgeoning tongue.
And now with state funding,
no use pretending it isn't hers.
She gives mutation for pleasure
the nod and her raspberry-sized taste buds
rake in the rent. A real crowd pleaser,
Rapunzel's unexpected out-doer."

Daily my fluctuating charmer
rolls royally from its bulwark:
a docile, bloated predilection.
Yet teenagers and dogs cry and hide,
shivering at the injustice. "No,
no," friends say, "it's her shy animal,
naturally bunching in soft folds
like an injured ruffle." The outcrop
nests in moody saliva, lured out

only by flies. In summer my tongue
unpetrifies, stirs at their thrumming,
and masters the switch and quick strike
like the content tail of our last human hurrah.

Town Legend: Keeping Well

"Not fair," says Fast
shoving Vamp who smiles sweetly,
"Fair's his hair. Fairly faithful."
"I care for you," says Fast.
Vamp spits, "Enamored animal,
this is no lair." The echo is spare:
not *who will have him?*
but *how to keep him?*
Fall suspended at its knees. They know well
that wells freeze in winter.

A cry hollows the bucket. See dusk
calling them home. Be well.
Begin to see what Fast says,
"I care for you," is not Vamp's air.
Her wealth of wind kicked
to the kind drip of whispers,
"I care for you, I careen you."
Fast breathes on ice for drinking water.
Vamp, pisses for the same, calls her
a fake, "Don't fall, fake,"
rustling her wide-scented sleeves.

Vamp wants to throw a dog
down the well so she can save him.
Fast is growing her hair. Down the dim,
damp moss Vamp says, "Fair's square."
Fast grumbles, "Upstairs,
you'll hate everything
you cannot say," as she wills the air
down her well with this goodbye.
The sky whitens, whitens.
Vamp could care less—
her partial perfume
absorbed, lifted off her very wrists.

Called Up to Carpenter a New Tradition,
We Make Use of a Standard Round Table

Why are there so many lines and scratches here?

> One scratch corrects the capillary action of milk.

How many can it seat?

> Used to a forest, the table invites always another chair.

Is it tall enough for us to sit under its shadow?

> If we plant sod on our floor; if we never look down, fork-stabs grow faces.

What shall we place on the table's surface?

> As if euphoria were a woman resting on rock, with gloriously little else to do, she reads at the pace of sipping.

When will the graffiti begin to dupe us?

> This table is our creature. We must mother roundness. Fruit will roll off our flat-chested sister. We will catch the apples. Place them just so. Spray the arrangement with clean water.

Will the top freeze in winter?

> Like the island you choose mid-century. An old man glides in circles, hands lifted, gesturing an opera.

Is something thrown away anyone's to take?

> A neighborhood noise to sleep against will do in a pinch.

Who will it unite? What will it rekindle?

Long ago a migration claimed the alphabet in sequence; the slack assumptions gave way to frank furniture.

i. THE GLASS IS A HAND

What is being prepared for is found under the sign of transparency.

Seven paints peel off the window frozen shut;
the flowered curtain cracks
into 32 kinds of translucence; debris
breaks under the maid's swift hand.
Even the room's alien grace arrests us.
Even the head of a son with mustaches.
In every slumped bowl, opaque unguent jar,
float glass is the room striking its face south.
An itinerant flash finds the echo. An extra wind
ringing church bells to break the lightning.
What would it be if 103 bell-ringers fell
at their ropes? If no one could stop
seeing even in the dark? And outside
the glass, light runs through light
laughter like contagion; a reflector fixes
to wet spokes. Each bell has 11 pitches
that some can feel in their back teeth.
Each room holds its shut mouth,
the gown glows silver this time. Inside
the daughter's skirt is in perpetual twirl—
her hem has 11 long stitches. Each tree
branches smoke over the snow; the drawings
of the story of glass are not to scale.
What you see comes out of your mouth
grazing the window, opening it with the will of rock.

Every object has been drawn either bright or dark,
and all 23 good shadows fall away
from the bad ones: a leaking in
the narrow street as your flashlight
draws the rain to be a fat thousand
broken windows and wine pitchers ever after.
Inside someone reads by a freezer light.
Even the letters are the same size.
Even the radiator is a hand.
In every chandelier, there are hallways,
chinks of rooms. The crystal bowl is a red
skirt spinning with a girl inside;
the skirt is draining. You hate the smell
of any other water. What's drawn in
exhausts itself in your mouth;
the air was also drawn in miniature,
colored blue this time touching clouds
with tiny bright bells around their necks.
You loosen the light, lose yourself in it:
each fulgurite is lightning's bonework,
a glassy revealing of diameter and path.
Each tooth has 7 colors. Each fragment of burn
brings the 30 trees closer. *I could see
the picture building into what I was trying to say:*
a bike quickly through the storm, *Fulgura Frango.*

In the photograph you can't tell
a dog barks at the fingerless son;
bells are shaking the window's pebbled-water,
throwing their disease onto a green jar.
After 19 hours of cold roads,
the eye naturally invents a new color—
its fragments are flying around the porch;
they're all over her skirt in stitches in the garden
where 6 allergic birds have landed for melon.
What would it be if light became ice?
If the twirling kept something inside
the slight daughter? Her ankles and arches
are sayings. Even the red underskirts
reflect 31 pieces. Each work of fire
is revealed in rails and laughing.
Each charred hallway has 109 water streaks.
In every drawing room, 5 fans chase
the dust looking along the long windows
which repel all liquid rays. The sun
draws a collection of sand-glass on the sill
into a word. You say the letters one by one
as they are traced on your back. In water
the branch is a worried fan. If you cannot say it,
how else will you know that you see?
Even flies come to the eyeball for food.

NOTES

Fly Paper Palimpsest

All languages preserve the memory of the period during which we lived on flies. —Jean-Pierre Brisset (translated by Stephanie Lysyr and Stefan Sinclair)

As I enjoy food when I am not invited to dine, I am myself a fly. —Desiderius Erasmus (translated by R. A. B. Mynors)

Flies filter opportunity out of offal, carrion, and rot. In the slurry of sewage and garbage, the stench of flotsam, they find usefulness and so tidy and transform loathsome sites. If *an inoculated man has a little extra eye,* then the inoculated house has a little extra fly. The wily figure claims both settler and fugitive status. It cross-pollinates mythology and gossip; it sieves through memory and sensation; it gathers and disperses the diseases of domesticity; it loads its legs with life-sources. And a fly sticks to its paper or a newly painted windowsill. The following ge(r)ms have been carried and collected here:

They seek no wonder but the human face from John Keats

True and Obscure Definitions of Fly, *Domestic and Otherwise* from the 1971 *OED*

The tiger strikes, what will man not do? / The fly rises: Where will man not fly to? from Henri Michaux (translated by Richard Ellmann)

Lum in Lum Lake means standing water and to sail as in Sail Wheel is to circle round from G. M. Hopkins

The idea of movement is a material also from Mei-Mei Berssenbrugge

This is a beautiful world, it means what I say from F. T. Marinetti (translated by Antonio Facchino)

you beasts hissing over the face of this dead woman from Aimé
 Césaire (translated by Clayton Eshleman and Annette Smith)

Crying is bad for your face from Margaret Atwood

bees of the invisible from Rainer Maria Rilke (translated by Jane
 Bannard Greere and M. O. Herter)

The small raine downe can raine from Anonymous, circa 1300

gong-tormented from W. B. Yeats

To articulate is to joint from Mark Taylor

*Telling the particles of the clouds, the leaves, the water / What immor-
 tality is. That it is immortal* from Sylvia Plath

Prophets never enjoy a Darwinian edge from E. O. Wilson

*Tongue is the cause of my being here. . . . Tongue brought us here and
 tongue brought you here* from Beulah Tate (in *Negro Folk Tales in
 Michigan*)

What is being prepared for is found under the sign of transparency
 from Walter Benjamin

> *If the aim of philosophy is, as*
> *Wittgenstein claims, to show the fly the*
> *way out of the fly-bottle, then the aim of*
> *poetry is to convince the bottle that*
> *there is no fly*
> —Steve McCaffery

ACKNOWLEDGMENTS

Grateful acknowledgment is made to the editors of the following publications in which some of these poems first appeared:

American Letters & Commentary, Arshile, Barrow Street, Best American Poetry 1997, Black Warrior Review, Boulevard, Boston Review, The Colorado Review, Conjunctions, Denver Quarterly, Fence, Fine Madness, Five Fingers Review, The Germ, High Plains Literary Review, The Journal, The New Orleans Review, The New Republic, The Ohio Review, Ploughshares, Provincetown Arts, Rhizome, Sonora Review, Quarter After Eight, Virginia Quarterly Review, and *Volt.*

"Miraculous Panoptic Precipitations" is for Amy England and Catherine Kasper. "A Spell in 839 Letters" is for Tim Earley. Many thanks to them and to Rikki Ducornet, Kay Jenkins, Bin Ramke, Claudia Rankine, Cole Swensen, Josh Wiener, and Suzanne Wise. My appreciation and gratitude to Heather McHugh.

Thanks also to the Fine Arts Work Center in Provincetown, the Colorado Council on the Arts, and the Rocky Mountain Women's Institute for their support.